Scrum Master Certification Guide

Professional Scrum Master™ (PSM) Exam preparation guide and handbook

By CJ Pitts

About the PSM™ I Certification

Scrum.org is a leading certification body for Scrum, founded in 2009 by Ken Schwaber and Alex Armstrong.

Its main certification on Scrum, called PSM™ I (Professional Scrum Master ^{TM} level 1) is one of the most famous certificates in the Scrum community. It validates gained fundamental knowledge of the Scrum framework and its application.

The PSM I Exam is 80 multiple choice, multiple answer, and true/false questions. The duration of the exam is 60 minutes. The passing score is 85%. The exam costs $150 and you can take it online. You need to understand the official Scrum Guide (from Scrum.Org), which you will find very easy to read after reading this book.

This book helps you understand the Scrum Guide better, and easier

Introduction

What is Agile?

It is not possible in some projects to gather all the requirements upfront because of their extreme uncertainties. So we use an "adaptive" method instead of a "predictive" one, in which we only define and plan a short period in the future, create a working product, and use the product to understand the needs and use the feedback to plan further and add more functionalities to the product.

Adaptive methods are called Agile. There are many Agile frameworks. The most famous Agile framework is Scrum.

Agility is about project development, but they also explain a little about the project management aspects in such environments. However, remember that the main point of Agile frameworks is not providing a project management system, but a project development system.

When do We Need to Use Agile?

Agility is helpful when it's hard to define the product upfront, because we can't understand it entirely, or the customer keeps changing its mind. In those cases, if you try to use a predictive method with upfront plans, you will have many change requests, and it will decrease your productivity and increase time and cost.

When Can We Use Agile?

Agility is based on adaptation, which in turn is based on the capability of producing pieces of working product throughout the project and using that for receiving feedback from the end users or their representatives. The interim outputs should be working product, because otherwise we won't be able to receive real feedback.

The working product is always "incremental", which means we keep adding new features to it. The development should be "iterative", which means we should repeat the development processes (e.g. design) for each Increment.

We can only use Agile when the product has the capability to be developed iteratively and incrementally. Unfortunately, not every product has it. The best case for Agility is software development. It's also used in some research projects, and many programs (e.g. organizational change initiatives).

Agile Manifesto

In 2001, a group of software developers published a manifesto that has since been considered the core of all Agile methods.

We are uncovering better ways of developing software by doing it and helping others to do it.		
Through this work we have come to value		
Individuals and interactions	Over	Processes and tools
Working software	Over	Comprehensive documentation
Customer collaboration	Over	Contract negotiation
Responding to change	Over	Following a plan
That is, while there is value in the items on the, we value the items on the left more		

Table 1 - Agile Manifesto

Scrum is a simple way of realizing all of these values

The creators of Scrum, and other Agile frameworks/methodologies such as XP (eXtreme Programming), Crystal, and DSDM were among the people who composed the manifesto.

Scrum Myths – Fact vs Fiction
Myth 1 – The Scrum Master must be present at the Daily Scrum
According to the Scrum Guide, the Daily Scrum is owned by the Development Team. Scrum is built on the observation that product development is a complex endeavor. This complexity manifests in a high degree of unpredictability. Even within the scope of a single Sprint, things will probably not go as expected. A critical member of the team becomes sick during the Sprint. A high-priority bug is discovered that needs to be fixed right away. Or a new idea emerges that better addresses the Sprint Goal. Frequent communication within the Development Team is paramount to deal with these changes as they arise.

The Daily Scrum is one of the boundaries of Scrum, and provides the Development Team with at least one daily opportunity to synchronize work and plan for the day ahead. How will the team work together until the next Daily Scrum to meet the Sprint Goal? The output of the Daily Scrum consists of a daily plan and (potentially) adjustments to the Sprint Backlog that are needed to reach the Sprint Goal.

Although the Scrum Master can be present to help facilitate the Daily Scrum, this is not required. The Scrum Master ensures that a Daily Scrum takes place, but the Development Team is responsible for conducting the meeting. Outside of the Development Team and potentially the Scrum Master, no other people participate. If the Daily Scrum results in decisions that affect others (like the Product Owner), they can be consulted by the Development Team afterward.

So, although the Scrum Master can participate during the Daily Scrum, this is certainly not required by Scrum.

Myth 2 – The sprint backlog cannot change during a sprint
The Sprint Backlog represents the work that a Development Team needs to pull from the Product Backlog to achieve the Sprint Goal. The Sprint Goal is an objective set by the Scrum Team during Sprint Planning and captures the hypothesis that the team wants to test, a goal it wants to achieve or an experiment to run. **Although the Sprint Goal is fixed during the Sprint, the Sprint Backlog is not.** This would be unwise considering the core premise of

Scrum: we can't create detailed plans for the future. Even if that future is a single Sprint, it is entirely possible that new insights or impediments emerge as the Development Team works through the Sprint Backlog.

A team might learn that a technology they picked does not perform as expected. Or a key feature needed to reach the Sprint Goal was missed during the Sprint Planning. As issues emerge, changes to the Sprint Backlog may be warranted in order to reach the Sprint Goal. The Development Team will then re-negotiate the Sprint Backlog with the Product Owner. **In short; a Sprint Backlog is flexible, as long as changes do not distract from the focus on the Sprint Goal.**

The Daily Scrum presents Development Teams with an excellent opportunity to inspect and adapt upon their progress to the Sprint Goal and make adjustments to the Sprint Backlog when deemed necessary.

Myth 3 – The Scrum Master must resolve every problem

The Scrum Guide clearly describes the various services that a Scrum Master provides. One of those is to remove impediments to the Development Team's progress. At first glance, this seems to support today's myth. But 'impediment' is an important keyword here. All too often, impediments are assumed to be whatever problems arise during the Sprint. But this is not the way how this responsibility should be understood.

What is an "impediment?
Impediments are those problems that hinder a Development Team's progress *and* lie outside of their capability to resolve on their own. This ties impediments strongly to another concept that is central to Scrum: self-organization. The background here is that – with software development being a very complex, unpredictable endeavor – it is likely for all sorts of unexpected problems to emerge during a Sprint. Examples of such unexpected problems are:

- Team members becoming sick
- problems with the development environment
- A broken laptop
- Unavailability of the Product Owner
- Conflict between team members
- Bugs in the production environment

Scrum

The Scrum Guide written by Ken and Jeff, they clearly describes Scrum as "a framework for developing and sustaining complex products"

Scrum consists of self-organizing, cross functional teams. Which simply means that the team consists of a group of people who each have different areas of expertise but work together for the same outcome. A project manager does control them since their expertise empowers them to make decisions collectively

The teams work in iterations, which allows the business the flexibility to change their requirements, but still gives the development team the certainty it needs to deliver a working product. This is one the most powerful things in relation to Scrum

Scrum takes its name from the analogy or rugby, where a team work together in a chaotic environment to keep control of a ball, this can be compared to a team working together in a chaotic environment to maintain control over a project

Scrum Theory

History repeats itself, unless you do something about it, or as Einstein put it, doing the same thing and expecting a different outcome is the definition of insanity.

Scrum is based upon empirical process control theory, the idea is simple, the name sounds complicated. It consists of three principles

- Transparency
- Inspection
- Adaption

The idea behind this, is that the Scrum team agree to be transparent (honest) in all that they do on the project

This transparency means that functionality is not done until it meets the development teams agreed definition of done. Transparency builds trust between the team members. Once the team has agreed on transparency, they agree to consistently check up on the progress (inspection) and make improvements based upon what they have seen (adaption). These can be improvements in practices, values, communication etc.

This is powerful, the ability to consistently inspect and adapt. Through this they are improving time and time again, before during and after the release of a product

Scrum Skeleton

The Scrum Skeleton is the simplest way to explain Scrum to someone using a very simple visual approach

The diagram is below and I will use it to give a simple explanation of Scrum

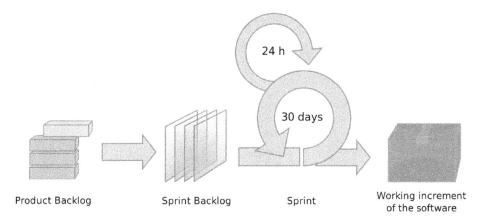

| Product Backlog | Sprint Backlog | Sprint | Working increment of the software |

Figure 1 - Scrum Skeleton

1. On the left hand side – the Product Backlog, which is essentially a list of the features and their acceptance criteria that the business desires from the product
2. The Sprint backlog is a subset of the product backlog, broken down into tasks and worked on in an iteration called a sprint
3. The sprint is between 2 weeks and 30 days (as recommended in the Scrum Guide) within the sprint the team will work the tasks to develop a working product
4. Within the sprint the daily scrum takes place at the same time and place. This meeting si for 15 minutes only
   a. The mini phases of the waterfall method occur within the sprint as seen below
      Requirement or specification gathering, Design, Develop, Test,
5. At the end of the sprint, the potentially shippable product\increment is delivered. The business can then review the increment within the sprint review and release the new product\increment if they choose to do so.
6. The team then openly discuss (supporting transparency) their progress during the sprint in a sprint retrospective (Supporting inspect) to ascertain how they can improve (supporting adapt) on any items or things that need improvement or retain things that going well.
7. This cycle then begins again and repeats until the product owner has no further items within the Product Backlog

This diagram represents the simplicity of the Scrum model as series of powerful mini factories that provide usable features at the completion of each sprint

Scrum Guide

The Scrum Guide which was written by Jeff Sutherland and Ken Schwaber, is the definitive guide to Scrum and the basis for the Professional Scrum Master Exam. The guide is the foundation for Scrum and from experience, this lack of understanding is what often leads to people or business not really understanding Scrum and therefore not implementing an actual version of Scrum that is aligned to the framework

Scrum - Framework or Process Methodology

The definition of Scrum is that it is a framework, not a process where it would essentially tell you in great detail how to build a product, it is actually a framework and it can be used to build complex products and it has the structure to support you or your organisation and bring the team together, ensure you are always inspecting progress and adapting, improving and delivering

The main thing to remember with Scrum, is to deliver often. However it is not the answer to all problems. There will naturally be things you will identify whilst using Scrum – gaps that need to be filled.

For example, within the software development process, test driven development is something that is sued in a large number of projects. Scrum does not say anything about this as a method, however it is widely used and recognised for its benefits to ensure you have a shippable increment or a high quality product

This is an example of how the Scrum is a framework as opposed to being a fully defined process. It is a framework within which you can employ various processes and techniques. It is important to remember this both in in real life and for the exam

The theory behind Scrum

Scrum is based upon Empirical Process Control Theory, and the important to note here is to learn from mistakes and improving, making new decisions, changes and adapting.

Remember Einstein "doing the same thing and expecting a different outcome is the definition of insanity"

Everything about Scrum is essentially about using the evidence from previous sprint to improve the future over and over again. This knowledge is essential if you aim to achieve the certification

Transparency – is about being open and honest as a team, admitting that when something is done, that this means it is complete and there is nothing left to deliver or to do. This is important, it is common on projects that there are situations where people do not feel confident enough to say something is not complete. This leads to problems further on into the project, where people think or believe a product is complete, when in actuality it is not. There may be a requirement for more testing, or additional features left to complete or build. This is why a common and agreed definition of "Done" is essential

In most scenarios, it may be that the product is not complete unless what has been built has been fully tested, all tasks are complete, it matches or meets the original designs etc. These are just a few things a team may decide. Additionally the Product Owner has acceptance criteria that must be met for each feature contained within the Product Backlog

Inspection and Adaptation – The team is constantly inspecting the and adapting at the end of each sprint. However it should be noted that inspection should not be so frequent that is gets in the way of the work.

In essence, if you agree Sprint 3 will only be 1 day in length, this would probably not allow enough time for the team to build the product, a sprint of this length would essentially be short to allow the stages within the sprint to be completed.

From experience,, again less than week is too short for a sprint, a 2 week sprint is often a good starting point and middle ground allowing the scaleup to a 4 week or 30 day sprint. Based upon the Emirical Process Control Theory, setting the length of the sprint is crucial because this decides or dictates how often you can inspect and adapt the product

Scrum Events – Which are necessary

In the exam, they expect you to know what events make up Scrum, These events are:

1. The Sprint
2. Sprint Planning
3. Daily Scrum
4. Sprint Review
5. Sprint Retrospective

These 5 events are considered mandatory within Scrum and the Scrum Guide. You can of course add to it, however you cannot take any of the 5 events away.

You essentially need to be planning, having a daily scrum for coordination, having a sprint review to ensure stakeholders are having conversations with the team and providing feedback into the next sprint, and having a retrospective to ensure you constantly improving

If you take any of these 5 events away, you are not doing Scrum. This is often missed because people or organisations again do not understand the fundamentals or foundations of Scrum.

Scrum Roles

Scrum Team

There are three roles in a Scrum project. There should be no further roles defined, because it is harmful to the unity of the team, and it is not compatible with the philosophy of Scrum.

A *Scrum Team* consists of the following three roles:

Product Owner	Scrum Master	Development Team
1 person	1 person	3 to 9 people
Full or part time	Full or part time	Full time (Highly recommended)
Business orientated	Scrum coach, facilitator	Specialist roles\skills

The term "Scrum Team" refers to all the project team members: everyone internal to the project. Scrum Team members usually have only one of the three standard roles of Scrum: Product Owner, Scrum Master, or Development Team member. It is possible for a single person to be assigned to more than one of the standard roles, but it is not recommended.

Other persons can also be involved in the project but they are not considered *internal* to the project and Scrum theory does not have much to say about them. They should have a certain set of behaviors though, to make it possible for a Scrum project to succeed.

The customer should understand and adopt the Scrum framework too, as the relation between the customer and the performing organization, and the way we deliver the project completely changes when we switch to the Scrum framework.

Note: in case of internal projects, the term "customer" will refer to another part of the company that orders the product and will probably use it in their operation afterward. The Scrum Team has two essential characteristics:

- **Self-organized**: The Scrum Team manages its own efforts rather than being managed or directed by others. In traditional methods, management efforts are separated and centralized; a subset of the project team is responsible for project management and others are only responsible for specialist activities. However, management and specialist efforts are *not* separated in Scrum.

- **Cross-functional**: The Scrum Team has all the expertise and competencies needed to get the job done without any help from outside the team.

These two characteristics are designed to optimize flexibility, creativity, and productivity, needed for the Agile environment of Scrum.

It might be required to have more team members for larger projects. In that case, we can use multiple teams for a single product, and it is called scaled Scrum. Scaled Scrum should follow the whole Scrum framework nevertheless.

The Product Owner

Each project needs a business oriented person, aimed at maximizing the value of the product and the work of the Development Team. In Scrum, this person is called Product Owner. Product Owners are normally a person from the supplier company, rather than from an external customer. In other words, Product Owner is NOT the customer's representative.

This role belongs to one person. There can be a committee to handle the responsibilities of this role, but in such a case, there should be one person representing this committee and we call this one person the Product Owner. There's only one Product Owner, even if you are using scaled Scrum with multiple teams.

They do not need to have application area knowledge of the project; they are focused on the business aspect. In software development projects for example, Product Owners do not need to be developers themselves; they just need to know a little about development, but a lot about how the business operates.

The Product Owner is responsible for the *Product Backlog*. The Product Backlog is a prioritized list of items (usually user stories) that the customer expects from the project; this is the main planning tool in Scrum. It is also the responsibility of the Product Owner to make sure that each Product Backlog item is easy to understand for the Scrum Team, and other stakeholders.

Product Owners should communicate effectively with the customer (the inevitable success factor in every project), and use the information to keep the Product Backlog updated with all the changes. They also measure the performance of the project, forecast the completion date, and make this information transparent to all stakeholders.

Product Owners understand the business, so they can rank each Product Backlog item based on its return on investment, as well as any other factors they find suitable for the business point of view of the project. The items will be sorted based on their *value*, so the higher they are on the list, the sooner they will be developed by the Development Team.

The entire organization must respect the Product Owner decisions for the project to be successful. No one should allow themselves to try to override those decisions, and no one should tell the Development Team what item to deliver, except for the Product Owner. A Product Owner's decisions might be influenced by others, but s/he must have the final say.

A Product Owner might delegate some of her/his responsibilities (such as preparing the list of items for the Product Backlog) to the Development Team, but stays accountable for them.

Remember, there's only one Product Owner, even in scaled Scrum; because it is very hard to manage value otherwise.

The Scrum Master

Scrum Masters are those who fully understand Scrum, and help the Scrum Team by coaching them, and ensuring that all Scrum processes are implemented correctly. The Scrum Master is a management position, which manages the Scrum process, rather than the Scrum Team. S/he is a servant-leader for the Scrum Team.

Besides ensuring that the Development Team understands and uses Scrum correctly, the Scrum Master also tries to remove impediments to the Development Team, facilitates their events, and trains and coaches them.

The Scrum Masters help the Product Owners too, by helping or consulting them on finding techniques, communicating information, and facilitating related events.

The responsibilities of the Scrum Masters are not limited to the Scrum Team. They should also help those outside the Scrum Team understand the appropriate interactions with the

Scrum Team to maximize the value created by the Scrum Team. The Scrum Master usually leads the organization in its effort to adopt Scrum.

It is possible for a single person to be both Scrum Master, and a member of the Development Team, although this is not recommended. Being a Scrum Master of a project might not occupy 100% of the time of a person; in this case, the best solution is to assign that same person as the Scrum Master in more than one project, rather than making them a member of the Development Team.

There's one Scrum Master role per team in scaled Scrum However, a single person can be the Scrum Master of more than one team.

The Development Team

Members of the Development Team are application area experts that are responsible for delivering backlog items, *and* managing their own efforts.

They should be cross-functional; being capable of doing the A to Z of the creation of each Product Backlog item. They should be self-organized: find their own way instead of receiving orders. They should be aligned with the goal of the project instead of working blindly. A task might be assigned to a single member throughout the Sprint, but the whole Development Team will be responsible and accountable for that task; no individual owns any task.

The Development Team delivers the final product of the project in step by step Increments, as defined in the Product Backlog. They always work in a product-based way.

It is highly recommended for members of the Development Team to work full-time on a single project, to stay focused and agile. The composition of the Development Team should not change so often. If there is a need to change team members, then this change should not happen during a Sprint. There will be a short-term decrease in productivity when the composition of the team changes.

Scrum is mostly effective when there are 3 to 9 Development Team members. For large projects, we can use a scaled model with multiple Scrum Teams.

Other Roles and Titles

You might have the temptation to give Development Team members more specific titles, such as designer, tester, quality inspector, and team leader; but Scrum does not allow this.

All members should have the same role, and the same title: Development Team member. Scrum is completely depended on collaboration and team-work. Development Team members should be united and completely aligned with the goal of the project. If you give them different titles or roles, they will focus on their own specific role in the project instead, and they might not pay enough attention to the final product which is necessary for Agile projects.

Each Development Team member is responsible for all the outputs created in the Development Team, even though each of them might be focused on a specific set of tasks.

So Who or where Is the Project Manager?

Now that we have reviewed all the Scrum roles, you might ask yourself, who is the *project manager*?

The answer is simple: there is no such role in Scrum; and none of the 3 roles of Scrum acts as a traditional project manager.

The project management responsibilities are *distributed* among the three roles of Scrum and there is no centralized project management in Scrum.

It is not against Agile to have a Project Manager, it's just not applicable to Scrum given the expectation is that the Project Manager role is distributed or shared among the three roles, Other Agile methods have Project Managers for example DSDM

Scrum Events
The Nature of Scrum Events

Figure 2 - Scrum Events

1. **Sprint**: Each Scrum project is a set of Sprints. A Sprint is a container for the four other events (as represented in the above diagram), development effort, and the maintenance of the Product Backlog.

2. **Sprint Planning**: Sprint Planning is the first event inside a Sprint. The Scrum Team plans the items they are going to deliver in the Sprint and the way they will deliver them.
3. **Daily Scrum**: The Development Team starts working on the objectives of the Sprint as soon as Sprint Planning is completed. During the Sprint, the Development Team holds a daily meeting, the Daily Scrum which normally lasts only 15 minutes. This is used to coordinate the work for the next 24 hours.
4. **Sprint Review**: Before the end of the Sprint, the Development Team reviews the outcome of the Sprint with the customer to receive feedback. The feedback is used to adjust the Product Backlog.
5. **Sprint Retrospective**: After the Sprint Review and just before the Sprint is over, the Scrum Team holds an internal meeting to review the Sprint (lessons learned) and use the feedback to improve the process in the next Sprint.

The four events inside the Sprint are designed to enable *Transparency, Inspection, regularity, and Adaptation*. We prefer to use these predefined meetings with fixed objectives and time-boxes (maximum durations) instead of ad-hoc meetings, which have the potential to waste our time.

There is an essential concept in Agile methods, called time-box: a predefined maximum duration of time. In order to maximize productivity, all the Scrum events must be time-boxed. It helps everyone focus on the real problems, instead of going into too much unnecessary detail.

The Time-Box Concept
The Time-box is an essential concept in Scrum. It is the way of staying focused and getting things done in an ever-changing environment. A time-box has a maximum duration in which we freeze the target and work on certain tasks or objectives.

The duration of a time-box Sprint should be agreed upon and fixed. We are free to change the duration based on lessons learned, but not frequently, and never based on single occasions.

For example,

- We are not allowed to say that "we have a lot to do this time, so let's increase the duration for this particular case".
- What we are allowed to say is "based on the previous ten Sprints, we've realized that the duration of our Sprints is unsuitable, and a 30% increase in duration might better fit our needs. So, let's increase it from now on".

The Sprint – Event 1

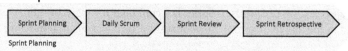

Figure 3 - Sprint - Event 1

Each Scrum project aims to deliver the product in a number of iterations, which are called Sprints in Scrum.

An Increment is developed in each Sprint. The definition of an Increment *"is a potentially releasable product"*.

An Increment is a sum of all Product Backlog items completed so far in a project and this Increment keeps getting bigger after each Sprint. You can think of it as different versions of a software; each time with more features.

Increments may or may not be actually released (put into use), but should always be potentially releasable

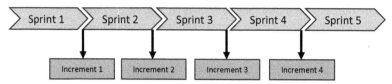

Figure 4 - Sprints

Customers usually request changes when they see the Increment (during the Sprint Review), and we note these new requests in the Product Backlog.

Sprint is a time-boxed event, which means we should fix its duration at the beginning of the project and not change it frequently or occasionally. Sprints are fixed for one month or less.

An important point is that we do not change the items of the Sprint Backlog after the Sprint is started and the plans are set. The Sprint Goal (discussed further in Sprint Planning) should not change either.

The Product Owner and the Development Team might try to clarify and re-negotiate the scope as more is learned about the items, by changing the tasks, but will not *change* the Sprint Backlog items and the Sprint Goal. Even the composition of the Development Team and the quality expectations should not change during a Sprint. These constraints are designed to make it possible to focus and get things done.

Each item in the Product Backlog should normally be completed in a single Sprint as this is much easier to manage. The Development Team selects a number of items from the top of the Product Backlog (this has already been prioritized by the Product Owner) and aim to get them "Done" (100% complete) during the Sprint. We want them to be really "Done" when the Sprint is over, and create an Increment.

An Increment is the sum of all the completed items during a Sprint and all previous Sprints. However, it's OK if they are not able to deliver all items. If they are pressured to deliver everything, they will start selecting fewer items to be safe, and it will consequently lower their productivity because of the "student syndrome". The student syndrome says that work expands to fill the available time.

It is important to agree on a definition of "Done" at the beginning of the project. We will not call something "Done", unless it fits the definition. A 99.999% completed item is not considered "Done", it would not be part of the Increment and it would not be demonstrated to the customer at the Sprint Review; it will be returned to the Product Backlog and if it's still at the top (after reprioritization), it will be selected for the next Sprint.

Sprint Time-boxes: Most companies use Sprint time-boxes of 2 to 4 weeks, although I have heard of sprints less than this, the Scrum Guide recommends 2 to 4 weeks. If we use Sprints longer than one calendar month, it will be likely for the unapplied changes to become large enough to create problems. This will increase the complexity and risk. Sprints should not be too short either, because we would not be able to produce complete Backlog items during it. Our goal is to deliver the final product item by item, inside the Sprints; we do not want to split a single Product Backlog item among several Sprints.

Can a Sprint be canceled? Even though Sprint Backlog items do not change, the Product Owner has the authority to *cancel* a Sprint. This can happen when the Sprint Goal becomes obsolete, due to changes in the Product Backlog, strategies, approach, market, etc. When a Sprint is canceled, the items that are "Done" will be reviewed and accepted, and the rest of the items (not started or partly complete) will be put back into the Product Backlog to be done in the future.

Sprint Planning – Event 2

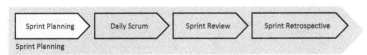

Figure 5 - Sprint Planning

The Development Team does not wait until the Product Backlog is 100% planned (all requirements are gathered and cleared) to start developing the project. As soon as the Product Backlog is mature enough (has the necessary number of stories) which will provide the information for the Sprint, the Scrum Team can start the first Sprint.

The first thing to do in each Sprint is Sprint Planning. Sprint Planning is a time-boxed meeting, usually fixed to 8 hours for a one month Sprint, or shorter for Sprints of less than a month. All three roles should attend this meeting.

The Development Team estimates the capacity of work it can deliver in a single Sprint. The Product Owner has already ranked and ordered the Product Backlog based on the business value of the items. The Product Owner also ensures that the items are easy to understand.

The Development Team then selects an appropriate number of items from the top of the Product Backlog, and puts them in the Sprint Backlog, to deliver in the current Sprint. The amount of work for each item is estimated by the Development Team and the total amount of work of the selected Product Backlog items is close to the estimated capacity of the Development Team.

The Scrum Team composes a Sprint Goal. The Sprint Goal is an objective that should be met within the Sprint through the implementation of the Product Backlog. The Scrum Goal provides guidance to the Development Team on why it is building the Increment.

The scope of the Sprint, which is made up of the items selected from the Product Backlog, needs more details through the Sprint. These details should be aligned with the Sprint Goal, and likely re-negotiations for them should be done in presence of the Product Owner.

When the items are selected and the Sprint Goal is agreed, it is time to plan how they will deliver the items into a "Done" product Increment and realize the Sprint Goal. This is the second element of the Sprint Backlog: tasks. Not all tasks are planned in this event; having a detailed plan for the first few days is enough. The Development Team can prepare detailed plans for the rest of the work later on. After all, Agility is about replacing upfront planning with adaptation.

A detail plan, is a breakdown of a Product Backlog item into detailed tasks needed to be done in order to create the item. Each task might have estimates, dependencies, and similar information to make tracking possible.

The Sprint Backlog will be ready at the end of this meeting and the Development Team should be able to describe what items they will deliver through the Sprint, and how they will do it.

Sprint Goal	To Do	Doing	Done
The goal of the sprint is to provide an online chat feature for the corporate website			
	Item 3 1.27		
	Item 5		

There is no specific rule in relation to documenting or presenting the Sprint Backlog, One of the more popular methods is the white board (as shown above)

Blue notes are items and the yellow sticky notes on the above board are tasks that are created by breaking down items. These tasks define what the Development Team will do to deliver each item, and they are responsible for preparing them. Some tasks are created at the Sprint Planning meeting, and some others throughout the Sprint.

The Sprint Backlog consists of the following:

- Selected items from the Product Backlog, to be delivered through the Sprint (they do not change during the Sprint)
- A detailed plan for turning the selected items into "Done" Increment of the product and to realize the Sprint Goal (they evolve during the Sprint)
- The Sprint Backlog elements are shown on the sample board above. The board can contain other elements such as the Sprint Goal, and a burn-down chart.

Items in the Sprint Backlog usually have the same order they had in the Product Backlog; therefore, the Development Team should work on the higher items first.

In scaled Scrum, members of all Development Teams will gather and select their items with agreement with the Product Owner. Each team has its own Sprint Backlog.

Daily Scrum – Event 3

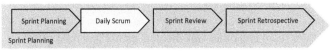

Figure 6 - Daily Scrum - Event 3

The Daily Scrum is a 15-minute meeting for the Development Team to inspect the work since the last meeting, and synchronize their work and plan for the next 24 hours. It must be held daily.

During the Daily Scrum, each member of the Development Team should answer these three questions:
1. What has been accomplished since the last meeting?
2. What will be done before the next meeting?
3. What obstacles are in the way?

Note: obstacles are not discussed in the meeting. If someone has a solution or concern, he should mention it after the Daily Scrum.

They assess progress toward the Sprint Goal and forecast the likelihood of completing the items *after* the Daily Scrum. The Daily Scrum is not a status meeting for all the stakeholders; it is just for the Development Team.

The Daily Scrum meeting should be held at the same time and place throughout the Sprint, to minimize complexity.

The Development Team should monitor Sprint progress each day, but not during the Daily Scrum. They can use a burn-down chart to track their remaining work and check to see if they are going to complete all items before the end of the Sprint. The information gathered through Daily Scrums would be useful for updating the board, but the updating is not done during the Daily Scrum

There's a common extra event in scaled Scrum: Scrum of Scrums. When Development Teams are done with their Daily Scrums, each will send a representative to a higher-level daily meeting called Scrum of Scrums. The representatives will synchronize team activities in this meeting. Each representative answers the three standard questions, plus this: what dependencies will your team have with other teams?

Sprint Review – Event 4

Figure 7 Sprint Review - Event 4

The duration of this meeting is normally **four hours** for a one month Sprint. If the Sprints are shorter then this meeting will be proportionally shorter. A good rule of thumb is 1 hour per week

At the end of the Sprint, the Scrum Team and other stakeholders gather and hold a four hour meeting to present the "Done" Increment to the customer. The demonstration is intended to collect feedback and raise change requests at the earliest time possible.

We welcome changes in Scrum and encourage them to be demanded, because it increases the satisfaction of the customer and will create a final product that better matches the needs of the customer.

This is the basis for adaptation: we use the Increments to understand the needs and plan further, instead of planning everything upfront.

The Development Team does not present an item, unless it is 100% complete based on the definition of "Done". The Product Owner makes sure (before the Scrum Review) that presented items are "Done". The Development Team demonstrates and explains the items.

The Product Owner discusses the status of the Product Backlog and the likely completion date based on the progress.

Finally, the whole Scrum Team collaborates on revising the Product Backlog based on the output of the Sprint and the feedback received from the customer.

Remember that Sprint Review is not a formal meeting for receiving approval from the customer; it's an informal meeting, without exchanging signatures, just aimed at receiving feedback and adjusting the Product Backlog.

Sprint Retrospective – Event 5

Figure 8 - Sprint Retrospective - Event 5

This meeting is normally **four hours** for a one month Sprint. If the Sprint is shorter than one month, this meeting will be proportionally shorter. As mentioned above, a good rule of thumb is 1 hour per week

After the Sprint Review and just before the end of the Sprint, another meeting will be held, aimed at process improvement (learning lessons), which is called Sprint Retrospective

There is a rule:

- We should always look for ways to improve. It does not matter how little the improvement is, there should be an improvement.

This meeting is a formal opportunity for improvement, even though we do not limit our improvement to the results of this meeting.

We will review (inspect) the Sprint, with regards to people, relationships, processes, and tools, and identify ways of improving them in the next Sprint.

Product Backlog Refinement

Besides the time-boxed events discussed before, there is an ongoing activity in Scrum projects called Product Backlog Refinement (Also known as Product Backlog Grooming).

It is the act of reviewing and revising Product Backlog items, which typically involves adding detail, estimates, and potentially reordering them.

The Product Owner is responsible for ordering (prioritizing) the items and the Development Team is responsible for estimating.

When the Product Owner adds a new item to the Product Backlog, s/he explains it to the Development Team and asks for estimates. Therefore, everyone knows the meaning of items before the Sprint Planning and the estimates are ready. During the Sprint Planning, the Development Team will review those pieces of information, just to make sure that everything is OK.

The main difference between this activity and the five Scrum events is that Scrum events are all time-boxed, while this is an ongoing activity that happens throughout the Sprint. However, it is important that this is managed. This activity should not consume more than 10% of the time of the Development Team.

Scrum Artifacts

Scrum artifacts are designed to increase transparency of information related to the delivery of the project, and provide opportunities for inspection and adaptation. They are management products useful for the creation of the specialist product of the project.

There are three artifacts in Scrum:

1. **Product Backlog**: An ordered list of everything that might be needed in the final product
2. **Sprint Backlog**: Selected items from the Product Backlog to be delivered through a Sprint, along with the tasks for delivering the items and realizing the Sprint Goal
3. **Increment**: The set of all the Product Backlog items completed so far in the project (up to the end of a certain Sprint)

And these are the extra concepts related to the artifacts:

- **Definition of "Done"**: The shared understanding of what it means for a piece of work to be considered complete
- **Monitoring Progress towards a Goal**: The performance measurement and forecast for the whole project
- **Monitoring Sprint Progress**: The performance measurement and forecasts for a single Sprint
- **Velocity**: a simple measurement for the average amount of work done during each Sprint.

Artifact 1 - Product Backlog

The Product Backlog is an ordered list of everything that might be needed in the final product of the project; in other words, parts of the expected final product (a wish list). All items are described in simple business language (non-technical) and all of them are presentable to every stakeholder. They should also be independent of each other, as we need to order them based on their business value. Every requirement and every change in the project will be reflected in the Product Backlog.

The Product Backlog is dynamically changing and improving; it is never complete. We do not wait until the Product Backlog is complete to start delivering the items; the first Sprint starts as soon as the Product Backlog has a sufficient number of stories.

The Product Owner sets a number of factors to determine the value of each item for the business (customer). Return on investment is usually one of the factors. All these factors will be summarized into business value (importance).

The Product Backlog items are ordered based on their value, in a way that the higher an item is, the sooner it will be delivered by the Development Team. As the items located at the top of the Product Backlog will be delivered sooner, they will also be more detailed and clear compared to the lower items.

Each Product Backlog item has a work estimate. These estimates are solely done by the Development Team, and are used in comparison to the capacity of the Development Team in a single Sprint, to determine the number of items that will be selected for that certain Sprint. Additional information might be added to each item to help the Scrum Team take control.

The Scrum Team should add details, estimates, and order to the Product Backlog items all the way through the project, which is called *Product Backlog refinement*. It should not consume more than 10% of the time of the Development Team.

The Product Backlog is created based on *discussion* rather than *documentation*. The Product Backlog items should be easy to understand for non-technical stakeholders.

The Product Backlog is a representation of the scope of the final product and therefore, there should be only one Product Backlog, no matter how many Scrum Teams are working on the project. This single concept also needs a *single* responsible person, so there's only one Product Owner.

Artifact 2 - Sprint Backlog

The Sprint Backlog is created during the Sprint Planning event which is the first event in a Sprint. During the Sprint Planning, the Scrum Team collaborates on creating the Sprint Backlog, which consists of the following:

- A number of items selected from the top of the Product Backlog, based on their estimated work and the estimated capacity of the Development Team
- A detailed plan for delivery of the items and realization of the Sprint Goal during the Sprint (tasks)

The Sprint Backlog items and the Sprint Goal do not change after the Sprint Planning and the Development Team will focus on delivering an Increment of "Done" based on this plan.

However, it is necessary to get more information, justify, or clear some of the items during the Sprint, which should be done in the presence of the Product Owner. The detailed plan (tasks) which is not complete at the end of the Sprint Planning, will continue to be updated as the Sprint continues. So, in general, some parts of the Sprint Backlog do not change during the Sprint, and the others do.

In scaled Scrum, each team needs its own Sprint Backlog.

Artifact 3 - Increment

An Increment is the sum of all completed Product Backlog items at the end of a Sprint. Each Increment must be "Done", which means it should be potentially releasable/shippable and usable by the end user. The Product Owner may or may not release a certain Increment, but it should be releasable nevertheless.

Note that the Increment concept is cumulative: each Increment also contains the features of the previous ones.

When multiple teams are working on the same product, each team produces a "Done" Increment. The Increments will be combined and create "one" Increment for the project.

The Definition of "Done"

There should be a shared understanding of what it means for a piece of work to be "Done".

This definition of "Done" must be discussed and agreed upon by the Scrum Team at the beginning of the project so that future Increments would be releasable.

The definition of "Done" usually contains the following:

- Development processes (e.g. programming, testing, documenting)
- Non-functional features (e.g. security, maintainability, scalability)
- Quality criteria and acceptance criteria
- Any tolerances

When multiple Scrum Teams are working on a single project, it might not be possible to use the same definition of "Done" for all teams, because they might be working on items of different natures.

In such a case, each Development Team defines its own definition of "Done" and delivers its items based on that definition. However, the integration of those definitions of "Done" should be capable of creating a potentially releasable Increment in the project level. Normally, we expect the definition of "Done" to come from the organization level.

This works as the minimum constrains for the project, and then the developers can add more to the definition of "Done", to make it suitable for the project. When there is not a definition of "Done" in the organization, the whole concept is defined by the Development Team.

Monitoring Progress Toward a Goal

The Product Owner is responsible to monitor the progress of the whole project toward its goal. This should be done at least once per Sprint Review. The Product Owner determines the amount of remaining work and compares it to the remaining work of the previous Sprints, and forecasts the completion date of the project. All stakeholders should have access to this information.

It's common to use a burn-down chart to visualize the progress of the whole project. The project burn-down chart shows the amount of **remaining work**, instead of the amount of completed work; therefore, the line for actual performance goes downward as we proceed and the faster it goes down, the happier we will be!

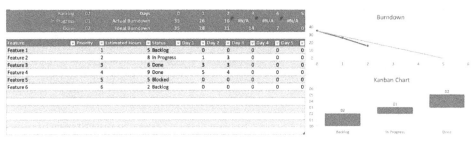

Figure 9 - Burndown Chart

The vertical axis (remaining work) shows the amount of work (which is a sum of all the estimates for each item in the Product Backlog), and the horizontal axis shows the amount of time passed from the beginning of the project or the number of Sprints passed.

It's also common to add a trend-line to the burn-down chart, to get a rough estimate of the completion date. This estimate is based on the assumption that no new items will be added to the Product Backlog and the development capacity will stay the same. It's expected from a Product Owner to only use this as a guide, and come up with a more reliable forecast for the completion date

Monitoring Sprint Progress

Besides the monitoring done for the whole project, we should also monitor the progress of each single Sprint throughout its life. This is the responsibility of the Development Team and should be done at least once per Daily Scrum. This information is used to calculate the likelihood of achieving the Sprint Goal and completing all items of the Sprint Backlog.

The Sprint progress information can be represented by a burn-down chart, and this chart can be a part of the Sprint board, where everyone can see

Scrum Revision

Agile Manifesto

In 2001, a group of software developers (while on a skiing vacation) published a manifesto that has since been considered the heart of all Agile methods. Scrum is a way of realizing this manifesto.

The complete Agile manifesto is as follows:

We are uncovering better ways of developing software by doing it and helping others to do it.		
Through this work we have come to value		
Individuals and interactions	Over	Processes and tools
Working software	Over	Comprehensive documentation
Customer collaboration	Over	Contract negotiation
Responding to change	Over	Following a plan
That is, while there is value in the items on the, we value the items on the left more		

Figure 10 - Agile Manifesto

Daily Scrum

The Daily Scrum is a time-boxed 15 minute meeting for the Development Team to inspect the work since the last meeting, and synchronize their work and plan for the next 24 hours. It must be held on a daily basis, at the same time and same place wherever possible (for example the Microsoft Agile teams hold theirs in a corridor with a projector).

During the Daily Scrum, each member of the Development Team should answer these three questions:
1. What has been accomplished since the last meeting?
2. What will be done before the next meeting?
3. What obstacles are in the way?

The Daily Scrum meeting should be held at the same time and place throughout the Sprint, to minimize the complexity. It is just for the Development Team; it is not a status meeting for all the stakeholders.

The Development Team should also monitor Sprint progress each day and therefore it is a good idea for the Sprint board (wall chart) to be visible during the Daily Scrum meeting. They can use a burn-down chart to track their remaining work and check to see if they are going to complete all items before the end of the Sprint.

Definition of Done

There should be a shared understanding of what it means for a piece of work to be "Done". This definition of "Done" must be discussed and agreed upon by the Scrum Team at the beginning of the project so that future Increments would be releasable.

When multiple Scrum Teams are working on a single project, it might not be possible to use the same definition of "Done" for all teams, because they might be working on items of different natures. In such a case, each Scrum Team will define its own definition of "Done" and delivers its items based on that definition. However, the integration of those definitions of "Done" should be capable of creating a potentially releasable Increment in the project level.

Development Team

The "Development Team" is one of the three roles defined in Scrum. Members of the Development Team are application area experts that are responsible for delivering backlog items, and managing their own efforts.

They should be cross-functional; being capable of doing the A to Z of the creation of each Product Backlog item. They should be self-organized; find their own way instead of receiving orders. They should be aligned with the goal of the project instead of working blindly. A task might be assigned to a single member throughout the Sprint, but the whole Development Team will be responsible and accountable for that task; no individual owns any task.

The Development Team delivers the final product of the project in step by step Increments, as defined in the Product Backlog. They always work in a product-based way.

It is highly recommended for members of the Development Team to work full-time in a single project, to stay focused and agile. The composition of the Development Team should not change so often. If there is a need to change team members, then this change should not happen during a Sprint. There will be a short-term decrease in productivity when the composition of the team changes.

Scrum is mostly effective when there are 3 to 9 Development Team members. For large projects, we can use a scaled model with multiple Scrum Teams. However, the use of multiple teams is not common in Scrum but you need to be aware of this.

Increment

An Increment is a sum of all completed Product Backlog items at the end of a Sprint. Each Increment must be "Done", and must be releasable. The Product Owner may or may not release a certain Increment, but it should be releasable (shippable).

Monitoring Progress Toward a Goal

The Product Owner is responsible to monitor the progress of the whole project toward its goal. This should be done at least once per Sprint Review. The Product Owner determines the amount of remaining work and compares it to the remaining work of the previous Sprints, and forecasts the completion date of the project. All stakeholders should have access to this information.

The project burn-down chart shows the amount of remaining work, instead of the amount of completed work; therefore, the line for actual performance goes downward as we proceed and the faster it goes down, the happier we will be!

Monitoring Sprint Progress

Besides the monitoring done for the whole project, we should also monitor the progress of each single Sprint throughout its life. This is the responsibility of the Development Team and should be done at least once per Daily Scrum. This information is used to calculate the likelihood of achieving the Sprint Goal and completing all items of the Sprint Backlog.

The Sprint progress information can be represented by a burn-down chart, and this chart can be a part of the Sprint board, where everyone can see.

Product Backlog

The Product Backlog is an ordered list of everything that might be needed in the final product of the project, in other words parts of the expected final product (a wish list).

All items are described in simple business language (non-technical) and all of them are presentable to every stakeholder. Every requirement and every change in the project will be reflected in the Product Backlog.

The Product Backlog is dynamically changing and improving; it is never complete. We do not wait until the Product Backlog is complete to start delivering the items; the first Sprint can be started as soon as the Product Backlog has a sufficient number of stories defined.

The Product Owner sets a number of factors to determine the value of each item for the business. Return on investment is usually one of the factors. All these factors will be summarized into one value (importance) and this is shown with each item.

The Product Backlog items will then be ordered based on their value, in a way that the higher an item is, the sooner it will be delivered by the Development Team. As the items located at top of the Product Backlog will be delivered sooner, they will also be more detailed and clear compared to the lower items.

Each Product Backlog item also has a work estimate. These estimates are solely done by the Development Team, and are used in comparison to the capacity of the Development Team in a single Sprint, to determine the number of items that will be selected for that certain Sprint. Additional information might be added to each item to help the Scrum Team take control.

Product Backlog Refinement (Grooming)

Besides the time boxed event discussed before, there is also an ongoing activity in Scrum projects called Product Backlog grooming. It is the act of reviewing and revising Product Backlog items, which typically involves adding detail, estimates, and order to them. The Product Owner is responsible for ordering (prioritizing) the items and the Development Team is responsible for estimating those items.

The main difference between this activity and the five Scrum events is that Scrum events are all time-boxed, but grooming is an ongoing activity that happens throughout the Sprint. This activity should not consume more than 10% of the time of the Development Team.

Product Owner

The Product Owner is one of the three roles defined in Scrum.

Each project needs a business oriented person, aimed at maximizing the value of the product and the work of the Development Team. In Scrum, this person is called Product Owner. Product Owners, like the two other roles, are from the performing organization, rather than from the client.

This role belongs to one person. There can be a committee to handle the responsibilities of this role, but in such a case, there should be one person representing this committee and we call this one person the Product Owner.

They do not need to have application area knowledge of the project; they are focused on the business aspect. In software development projects for example, Product Owners do not need to be developers themselves, they just need to know a little about development, but a lot about how the business operates.

The Product Owner is responsible for the Product Backlog. The Product Backlog is a prioritized list of items (aka stories or user stories) that the client expects from the project; this is the main planning tool in Scrum. It is also the responsibility of the Product Owner to make sure that each item (user story) is easy to understand for the Scrum Team, and other stakeholders.

Product Owners should communicate effectively with the customer (the inevitable success factor in every project management method), and use the information to keep the Product Backlog updated with all the changes. They also measure the performance of the project, forecast the completion date, and make this information transparent to all stakeholders.

Product Owners understand the business, so they can rank each Product Backlog item based on its return on investment as well as any other factor they find suitable for the business point of view of the project. The items will be sorted based on their value, so the higher they are on the list, the sooner they will be developed by the Development Team.

The entire organization must respect the Product Owner decisions for the project to be successful. No one, even the CEO, should allow themselves to try to override those decisions, and no one should tell the Development Team what item to deliver, except for the Product Owner who sets and orders the items. A Product Owner's decisions might be influenced by others, but he/she must have the final say.

A Product Owner might delegate some of his/her responsibilities (such as preparing the list of items for the Product Backlog) to the Development Team, but stays accountable for them.

Project Manager

Scrum projects do not have a role called "project manager".

Some people consider the Scrum Masters to be the equivalent to traditional project managers; but it is not true, because the Scrum Master responsibilities are very different than a traditional project manager.

So, a better question to ask is: what happens to project management?

The project management responsibilities are distributed among the three roles of Scrum and there is no centralized project management in Scrum.

Scrum Master

The Scrum Master is one of the three roles defined in Scrum.
Scrum Masters are those who fully understand Scrum, and help the Scrum Team by coaching them, and ensuring that all Scrum processes are implemented correctly. The Scrum Master is a management position, which manages the Scrum process, rather than the Scrum Team. He/she is a servant-leader for the Scrum Team.

Besides ensuring that the Development Team understands and uses Scrum correctly, the Scrum Master also tries to remove impediments to the Development Team, facilitates their events, and trains and coaches them.

The Scrum Masters help the Product Owners too, by helping or consulting them on finding techniques, communicating information, and facilitating related events.

The responsibilities of the Scrum Masters are not limited to the Scrum Team. They should also help those outside the Scrum Team understand the appropriate interactions with the Scrum Team to maximize the value created by the Scrum Team.

The Scrum Master usually leads the organization in its effort to adopt Scrum.
It is possible for a single person to be both Scrum Master, and a member of the Development Team, although this is not recommended. Being a Scrum Master of a project might not occupy 100% of the time of a person; in this case, the best solution is to assign that same person as the Scrum Master in more than one project, rather than making them a member of the Development Team.

Scrum Team

There are three roles in a Scrum project; no less, and no more. We are not allowed to define any other roles, because it is harmful to the unity of the team, and it is not compatible with the philosophy of Scrum.

A Scrum Team consists of the following three roles:
- Scrum Master
- Product Owner
- Development Team

The term "Scrum Team" refers to all the project team members: everyone internal to the project. Scrum Team members usually have only one of the three standard roles of Scrum: Product Owner, Scrum Master, or Development Team member. It is possible for a single person to be assigned to more than one of the standard roles, but it is not recommended.

The Scrum Team is a part of the performing organization (the company which executes the project either for itself or as a contractor for an external customer).

Other persons can also be involved in the project but they are not considered internal to the project and Scrum theory does not have much to say about them. They should have a certain set of behaviors though (e.g. respect how a Scrum project works), to make it possible for a Scrum project to succeed.

The customer should understand and adopt the Scrum framework too, as the relation between the customer and the performing organization and the way we deliver the project completely changes when we switch to the Scrum framework.

The Scrum Team has two essential characteristics:
- Self-organized: The Scrum Team manages its own efforts rather than being managed or directed by others. In traditional methods, management efforts are separated and centralized; a subset of the project team is responsible for project management and others are only responsible for specialist activities. However, management and specialist efforts are not separated in Scrum.
- Cross-functional: The Scrum Team has all the expertise and competencies needed to get the job done without any help from outside the team.

These two characteristics are designed to optimize flexibility, creativity, and productivity, needed for the Agile environment of Scrum.

Sprint

Each Scrum project delivers the final product after a number of cycles, which are called Sprints. An Increment is developed in each Sprint. An Increment is a potentially releasable part of the final product. An Increment is a sum of all Product Backlog items completed so far in a project and this Increment keeps getting bigger after each Sprint.

Therefore you can consider each new Increment at the end of a Sprint to be an updated version of the previous Increment with new features and functionalities, which may or may not be actually released (put into use), but should always be potentially releasable.

Customers usually request changes when they see the Increment (during the Sprint Review), and we note these new requests in the Product Backlog.

Sprint is a time-boxed event, which means we should fix its duration at the beginning of the project and not change it frequently or occasionally. Sprints are usually fixed for one month or less.

An important point is that we do not change the items of the Sprint Backlog after the Sprint is started and the plans are set. The Sprint Goal (discussed further in Sprint Planning) should not change either. The Product Owner and the Development Team might try to clarify and re-negotiate the scope as more is learned as more is leaned about the items to be delivered, but will not change the Sprint Backlog. Even the composition of the Development Team should not change during a Sprint. These constraints are designed to make it possible to focus and get things done.

Each item (story) in the Product Backlog should normally be developed (completed) in a single Sprint as this is much easier to manage. The Product Owner and the Development Team select a number of items from the top of the Product Backlog (this has already been prioritized by the Product Owner) and aim to get them "Done" (100% complete). We want them to be really "Done" when the Sprint is over, and create an Increment. An Increment is the sum of all the completed items during a Sprint and all previous Sprints.

It is important to agree on a definition of "Done" at the beginning of the project. We will not call something "Done", unless it fits the definition. A 99.999% completed item is not considered as "Done", it would not be part of the Increment and it would not be demonstrated to the customer at the Sprint Review.

Sprint Time boxes: Most companies use Sprint time boxes of 2 to 4 weeks. If we use time-boxes longer than one calendar month for Sprints, it will be likely for the unapplied changes to become large enough to create problems. This will increase the complexity and risk. Therefore, we should keep the Sprints no more than one calendar month. Sprints should not be too short either, because we would not be able to produce complete Backlog items during it. Our goal is to deliver the final product item by item, inside the Sprints; we do not want to split a single Product Backlog item among several Sprints.

Can a Sprint be cancelled? Even though each Sprint is frozen and does not change, the Product Owner has the authority to cancel a Sprint. This can happen when the Sprit Goal becomes obsolete, due to changes in the Product Backlog, strategies, approach, etc. When a Sprint is cancelled, the items that are "Done" will be reviewed and accepted, and the rest of the items (not started or partly complete) will be put back into the Product Backlog to be done in the future.

Sprint Backlog
The Sprint Backlog is created during the Sprint Planning event which is the first event in a sprint. During the Sprint Planning event, the Scrum Team collaborates on creating the

Sprint Backlog, which consists of the following:
- A number of items selected from the top of the Product Backlog, based on their estimated work and the estimated capacity of the Development Team
- The Sprint Goal, which will help describe the real meaning of the items and direct the efforts of the Development Team
- A detailed plan for delivery of the items and realization of the Sprint Goal during the Sprint

The Sprint Backlog is frozen after the Sprint Planning and the Development Team will focus on delivering an Increment of "Done" based on this plan. The statement "the Sprint Backlog is frozen" means that items (stories) in the Sprint Backlog cannot be added or removed during the Sprint. However, it might be necessary to get more information, justify, or clear some of the items during the Sprint, which should be done in the presence of the Product Owner. The detailed plan which is normally not complete at the end of the Sprint Planning, will continue to be updated as the Sprint continues.

Sprint Planning

The Development Team does not wait until the Product Backlog is 100% planned (all requirements are gathered and cleared) to start developing the project. As soon as the Product Backlog is mature enough (has the necessary number of stories) which will provide the information for the Sprint, the Product Owner and the Development Team can start the first Sprint.

The first thing to do in each Sprint is Sprint Planning. Sprint Planning is a time-boxed meeting, usually fixed to 8 hours for a one month Sprint, or shorter for Sprints of less than a month. All three roles should attend this meeting.

The Development Team should estimate the capacity of work it can deliver in a single Sprint. The Product Owner has already ranked and ordered the Product Backlog based on the value of the items. The Product Owner also ensures that the items (stories) are easy to understand. The Development Team then selects an appropriate number of items from the top of the Product Backlog, and puts them in the Sprint Backlog, to deliver in the current Sprint. The amount of work for each item is estimated by the Development Team and the total amount of work of the selected Product Backlog items is close to the estimated capacity of the Development Team.

Following the selection of the items, the Scrum Team should draft a Sprint Goal. The Sprint Goal is an objective that should be met within the Sprint through the implementation of the Product Backlog. The Scrum Goal provides guidance to the

Development Team on why it is building the Increment.

The scope of the Sprint, which is made up of the items selected from the Product Backlog, might need to have more details through the Sprint. These details should be aligned with the Sprint Goal, and likely re-negotiations for them should be done in presence of the Product Owner. The Sprint Goal is also included in the Sprint Backlog.

When the items to deliver are selected and the Sprint Goal is agreed, it is time to plan how they will deliver the items into a "Done" product Increment and realize the Sprint Goal. This is the last part of the Sprint Backlog. The Sprint planning is not necessarily completed in this meeting; having a detailed plan for the first few days is enough; the Development Team can prepare detailed plans for the rest of the work later on.

A detail plan is a breakdown of a Product Backlog item into detailed tasks needed to be done in order to create the item. Each task might have estimates, dependencies, and similar information to make tracking possible.

The Sprint Backlog will be ready at the end of this meeting and the Development Team should be able to describe what items they will deliver through the Sprint, and how they will do it.

Sprint Retrospective

This meeting is normally three hours for a one month Sprint. If the Sprint is shorter than one month, this meeting will be proportionally shorter.

After the Sprint Review and just before the end of the Sprint, another meeting will be held, aimed at process improvement (learning lessons), which is called Sprint Retrospective.

There is a rule: we should always look for ways to improve. It does not matter how little the improvement is, there should be an improvement. This meeting is a formal opportunity for improvement, even though we do not limit our improvement to the results of this meeting. We will review (inspect) the Sprint, with regards to people, relationships, processes, and tools, and identify ways of improving them in the next Sprint.

Sprint Review

The duration of this meeting is normally four hours for a one month Sprint. If the Sprints are shorter then this meeting will be proportionally shorter.

At the end of the Sprint, the Scrum Team and other stakeholders gather and hold a four hour meeting to present and inspect the "Done" items (the Increment) from the current Sprint and adapt the Product Backlog by marking off "Done" items as complete and add new items or change the existing ones if necessary. The presentation of the Increment in this meeting is intended to collect feedback and raise change requests at the earliest time possible.

We welcome changes in Scrum and encourage them to be demanded, because it increases the satisfaction of the customer and will create a final product that better matches the needs of the customer.

The Development Team does not present an item, unless it is 100% complete based on the agreed definition of "Done". The Product Owner makes sure (before the Scrum Review) that presented items are "Done". The Development Team demonstrates and explains the items.

The Product Owner discusses the status of the Product Backlog and the likely completion dates based on the progress.

Finally, the whole Scrum Team collaborates on revising the Product Backlog based on the output of the Sprint and the feedback received from the customer.

Timebox

Time-box is an essential concept in Scrum. It is our way of staying focused and getting things done in an ever-changing environment. A time-box is a fixed period of time in which we freeze the target and work with full focus on certain tasks or objectives. Time-boxed events repeat many times, until the final goal of the project is achieved. All the changes are applied only when one time-box is finished and we are ready to start the next one.

The duration of a time-box should be agreed upon and fixed. We are free to change the duration based on lessons learned, but not frequently, and never based on single occasions. For example, we are not allowed to say that "we have a lot to do this time, so let's increase the duration for this particular case". What we are allowed to say is "based on the previous ten time-boxes, we realized that the duration of our time-boxes is not suitable, and a 30% increase in duration might better fit our needs. So, let's increase them from now on".

www.ingramcontent.com/pod-product-compliance
Lightning Source LLC
Chambersburg PA
CBHW070906070326
40690CB00009B/2013